THE PRICELESS PROJECT PRESENTS

CONFIDENCE TO GREATNESS
FOR
TEENAGE GIRLS

The Inspiration and Guidance to Succeed in Life

RUBY L. TAYLOR, M.S.W.

Confidence to Greatness
917 Columbia Avenue
Suite 123
Lancaster, PA 17603
www.ConfidencetoGreatness.org
Manufactured in the United States of America

Library of Congress Cataloging-in-Publication Data
Confidence to Greatness for Teenage Girls: The Inspiration and
Guidance to Succeed in Life / [compiled by] Ruby L. Taylor, M.S.W.
ISBN-13 978-0-97451-221-1 (trade paper)
ISBN-10 0-97451-221-4 (trade paper)

Contents

III: RELATIONSHIPS

IV: FAMILY ISSUES

V: LIFE LESSONS

VI: SELF-WORTH

VII: INSPIRATION AND RESOURCES

NOTES

Dear Priceless One,

The Confidence to Greatness Project originated in 2007 when I (Ruby L. Taylor) wrote a poem for my niece and other hurting students titled "What Am I Worth?"

WHAT AM I WORTH?

If my mother does not love me, am I worth love?
If my father does not protect me, am I worth protection?
If my family curses me and calls me names, am I worth respect and kindness?
If my teacher does not educate me, am I worth education?
If my community calls me a failure, am I worth success?

WHAT AM I WORTH?

I am worth the love of the Universe, even if my mother is not capable of giving me that love.
I am worth the protection of the CIA, FBI and all of the military forces, even if my father is unable to protect me.
I am worth the highest respect and the greatest acts of kindness, even if my family is unable to treat me with love and care.
I am worth an Ivy League education and Fortune 500 training, even if my teachers are unable to prepare me for my bright future.
I am a success despite my failures.

WHAT AM I WORTH?
*Actually, **I AM PRICELESS**.*
My worth is so high that it cannot be valued and it cannot be bought.
WHAT AM I WORTH?
I AM PRICELESS!

—*Ruby L. Taylor*

I use this poem with hurting teenagers in Lancaster City, Pennsylvania, to help encourage each student to know that he/she is priceless. The poem and life experiences inspired me to empower female teens who are struggling with self-worth and achievement. The truth is, the hurt I saw in so many young women struck a chord with me because I had many struggles in my childhood and teenage years. Growing up in the Bronx, constantly fighting with my sisters, being molested, and surviving the murder of my brother created many difficulties in my life. Through it all, I have grown, healed, and I can say today that I AM PRICELESS, no matter what. It is my dream that every young woman will know that she is PRICELESS, no matter the circumstances. This book is guaranteed to increase your priceless spirit and give you confidence to GREATNESS.

—*Ruby L. Taylor, M.S.W.*

Follow Us on Twitter @WeArePriceless1
Like Us on Facebook www.Facebook.com/PricelessProject

INTRODUCTION

About The Author

Ruby Taylor is an author and social worker from the Bronx, N.Y., and she currently lives and works in Lancaster, Pa. She is the self-proclaimed world's greatest aunt and godmother. Ruby is a mentor to many young women and young men. She has worked in Baltimore, Md., Richmond, Va., Washington, D.C., and New York City. Ms. Ruby, as she is affectionately called, graduated from Howard University and Virginia Union University. She enjoys traveling, and her favorite places to visit are San Juan, Puerto Rico, and San Diego, California. Ruby is on a mission to let every young woman know she is beautiful and priceless.

Hi Priceless One,

Before you get started, please take the time to complete the PRICELESS SELF-WORTH QUIZ. Find out your current score before you read the book and then see where you are after you finish the book. You may be surprised.

Circle the answer that best describes you today.

1. I am beautiful
   Never   1
   Sometimes   2
   Most of the time   3
   Always   4
2. I allow others to influence my decisions
   Never   1
   Sometimes   2
   Most of the time   3
   Always   4
3. I love my life
   Never   1
   Sometimes   2
   Most of the time   3
   Always   4
4. In order for me to be happy, I need to change
   Nothing (I am already very happy)   4
   Some things in my life   3
   A lot of things in my life   2
   All of the things in my life   1

5. When people see me, they see someone who is

Pretty, Happy, Successful	4
Attractive, OK, Striving	3
Unattractive, Sad, Trying	2
Ugly, Mad, Failure	1

6. I am Priceless

Never	1
Sometimes	2
Most of the time	3
Always	4

7. When I need support, I turn to my family or friends

Never	1
Sometimes	2
Most of the time	3
Always	4

Once you've completed the quiz, add up all of the numbers assigned to each response you chose and review the appropriate feedback below.

If Your Score Ranged From:

SCORE 7-13 PRICELESS VALUE: IN DANGER

Your score indicates that you rely heavily on other people's opinions and have a low sense of your true value. (Don't worry. Your self-worth can always increase.) You are focusing too much on the negative and disregarding the many positive aspects you bring to your life and others. At times, you find it hard to assert yourself. When and if you reward yourself, you will often do it in self-destructive ways. It is important that you take time to feed and nurture your inner being. Start increasing your self-worth first by telling yourself throughout the day that you are PRICELESS. You are worthy of love, happiness, peace, blessings, forgiveness, and kindness. Learn more ways to increase your self-worth by reading the stories and tips found in this book.

SCORE 14-20 PRICELESS VALUE: MODERATE

Your score indicates that your priceless value is high in some areas and low in others. You are very reliable and honor your commitments to others. When things go wrong in your life, you often blame yourself and do not ask for support/help from others. (Don't worry. Your self-worth can always increase.) You are supercritical of yourself, and at times, you need to give yourself a much-needed break. You do manage to find areas of your life that satisfy you and give you inner happiness. Learn more ways to increase your self-worth by reading the stories and tips throughout this book.

SCORE 21-27 PRICELESS VALUE: GOOD

Your score indicates that you know who you are and what you need to be happy. You have a good sense of your priceless value. You are always working on being the best you can be. You surround yourself with supportive friends and/or family. You see your strengths, but you may need to learn to work with your weaknesses. (Don't worry. Your self-worth can always increase.) To help maintain your priceless value, read the stories and tips throughout this book

SCORE 28 PRICELESS VALUE: EXCELLENT

You have a deeply developed sense of self and are self-nurturing. You respect your own feelings as well as those of others. When you are in need of support, you are willing and able to turn to friends or family for comfort. You are patient with yourself. You lead a healthy, well-balanced life. To maintain your PRICELESS value, learn more ways to increase your self-worth through the contents of this book.

Self-Worth Defined

By Barb Steinberg

- What is self-worth? Self-worth is having confidence, believing in yourself, and liking yourself. Self-worth is knowing that it is because of WHO you are and not what you DO that you are worthy. You are worthy of being alive; you are worthy of being liked/loved; and you are worthy of good things happening in your life.

- How does body image impact the female priceless spirit? Your priceless spirit already knows that you are more than just a body. Your body is your outer shell, the part that people see at first glance; but if those people spend a little bit of time with you, they will get to know who you really are, beyond your curly hair, your short legs, your green eyes, etc. Your spirit already knows that you are beautiful and special and perfect—exactly how you are. In the eyes of your spirit, you don't need to change your body one bit.

Your spirit wants you to be happy with how your body looks today. Therefore, begin right now to say kind things to yourself, such as "I like my short hair. I like my big, brown eyes. I like that I am tall. I like that I have strong legs that can run fast." With every kind word you say about yourself, you will feel better and better. Practice this technique in front of your mirror every day. It works!

- Barb Steinberg is a licensed, master's level, clinical social worker. She has worked with adolescents—and the adults in their lives—for more than 20 years through life coaching, workshops, parent education, and products, such as her popular educational DVD *The Wisdom of Girls: Teens, Sex & Truth.* Her clients include The Girls School of Austin, The Griffin School, The Khabele School, The Girls Empowerment Network, and many more. She has been featured online at savvysource.com and livemom.com and in broadcast media on KVUE-TV and Fox7 in Austin, Texas, as an expert on adolescent girl issues. http://www.barbsteinberg.com.

Queen

By Kimberly Gray

Green, brown or beautiful blue,
Windows to the soul of a temple called you,
Golden-blonde, black or brown,
Kinks, coils and curls are your God-given crown.
Curvy, boxy or lean as a pole,
Beauty exudes from your crown to your soles,
Your athletic, creative, and technical glory,
Are history's next, greatest-told story.
So, step forth, young queens,
Step bold, step tall,
The universe awaits,
And it's your name being called.

Notes

I

HURT, PAIN, and HEALING

Through The Storm

By Melissa Carter-Coleman

Beautiful, blessed, favored, masterpiece, worthy, and priceless are words I never knew described me. If I had never gone through any difficulties, I still would not have known.

Only after all of my trials and tribulations can I say and believe that I am 100 percent PRICELESS.

It is my hope that you do not have to go through the life experiences I had to face in order to know and appreciate your self-worth. You are beautiful, worthy and PRICELESS today, now, and forever.

My life story begins with me being born to a young mother. My mom had her first child at the age of 18. When she met my father, he was 20 years older. My father was very abusive to her; and even with the abuse, she had three children with him. By the time I was 5, my mother had five children. When I was 6 years old, my mother left us with our dad. My father was responsible for the three of us he had with my mother. She took my youngest and oldest brothers and moved to Bridgeport, Conn., and left us in Lancaster, Pa.

Throughout my childhood, no one told me about my self-worth. I lived as though I had no care in the world. I missed my mom, and no matter how much people spoke badly about her, in my eyes, she did nothing wrong. Growing up, we stayed with family from time to time, and were thought of as the black sheep of the family. The treatment from our family and my longing to be with my mother left a void in my life.

My teenage years consisted of experimenting with drinking alcohol, using marijuana, and having sex. At 15 years old, my baby's father was not interested in our pregnancy. We lived in separate states, and it made it easier for him not to be an active father. By the time I was 16, I was a teenage mother raising my daughter alone. When I was 17, I found myself in an abusive relationship with a man who used drugs. By the time I was 21, I had three children. I depended on my man and the welfare system to take care of me. We lost apartment after apartment and my life was pure chaos. My life was confusing, insane, and out of control.

My life took a turn for the worse, when my man made a statement: "I know how we can make money." And I asked that fatal question: "How?" The answer: "We can sell drugs." He knew where to buy the drugs because he was already buying drugs regularly. We began selling crack; and before I knew it, I was selling drugs to the drug dealers. I would get my cocaine cooked up and bagged and took cabs to people's houses. The more money I made, the more money and drugs my man would take. The insanity grew; my relationship and life got worse.

In January 1993, my house was raided and my whole body went numb. I did not know what to think. They arrested my man and me and took us to the police station, where we were questioned and charged with possession with intent to deliver and with conspiracy. On March 14, 1995, I was sentenced to a mandatory three to six years in a state correctional institution. I was given six days to pack my stuff, find a place for my children, and turn myself in to the authorities. March 20 came so fast. I had to report to the Lancaster County prison, and reality set in. What was I going to do? How did my life get so out of control? I spent two weeks in the county prison and then went upstate to get my classification and determination of where I would spend my sentence.

I was classified a level two, and that meant minimal security. I was sent to SCI (State Correctional Facility) Cambridge Springs. My inmate number was OC 8840, and that was my identity until the time I was released. That number is still with me even though I am free; it is a constant reminder that keeps me grounded.

While in prison, I completed a host of classes: anger management, parenting, drug and alcohol, new choices, computer drafting, and building trades. I also did a lot of soul searching. I decided to end my relationship with my kids' father; that was the best decision I made. While I was in prison, I felt empowered; and for the first time since I was in the relationship, I felt free on the inside—even though I was incarcerated. Through my newly found spirituality, I knew that my life had changed for the better. My new choices gave me the opportunity to go home without being scared. I no longer feared being beaten up, nor was I too afraid to leave or afraid to do anything because my ex-man would be jealous.

Upon my release from prison, I went to a half-way house for one year. The caring staff there helped me learn to believe in myself and to view my priceless spirit. After that year, I moved in with my new boyfriend, who is now my husband. My life began anew, and I got married and had two more children. After my release, I watched my three older children graduate high school and my oldest graduate college. It was difficult adjusting to my new life, but I did it because I finally knew and appreciated myself. I knew I was priceless.

Why am I priceless? I am priceless because I am somebody; I am beautiful; and I have a voice. I deserve to be treated with respect, honesty, and dignity. I don't have to sell drugs. I don't deserve to be beaten. I can grow through my past. I now have a future full of dreams and hopes. Everything I went through gave me the ability to have a loving heart, a great personality, and priceless spirit. I embrace the fact that I am worthy of good things. My name is Melissa Carter-Coleman and I am PRICELESS. You are PRICELESS, too!

Gone But Never Forgotten

By Ruby L. Taylor, M.S.W.

Have you ever wished you could do things differently and/or say things differently? My July 1991 loss was the moment in which I wish I could have turned back the hands of time

I had just become 14, and I felt that I no longer needed my brother Daniel's constant guidance and approval. I was beginning to make my own decisions and find my own way, which caused major conflict in our relationship. Even in our conflict, we would patch things up just by being in each other's presence; and even though the word "sorry" was rarely spoken, we would be buddies again. In July 1991, we had a huge blowup, and I can remember his exact words. He said, "I'm not going to protect you when you get to high school. I am only going to protect Minerva." Those words pierced my heart, but I could not let him know that. My response was, "I don't need your protection." Who knew we wouldn't have an opportunity to say "sorry" without words. My brother was murdered August 4, 1991.

The inability to make things better with him made me sick with remorse. I felt guilty about our arguments because I could never say I was sorry to him and/or patch things up. Talking about this with my family was not an option, so I did other things that distracted me from my negative feelings, such as cutting class, cursing out the assistant principal, lying to my parents, and anything that came to my mind. I just wanted the negative feelings to disappear, but, they did not and I was in my own version of HELL.

Daniel and I were much more than brother and sister. He was the baby boy, and I am the baby girl in our family of 10. We were born and raised in The Bronx, New York, so we had to stick together and always looked out for each other. We were the quintessential best friends; we told each other our innermost secrets and went everywhere together. We rode our bikes together or better yet, I followed him everywhere he would let me go. I remember playing basketball, Nintendo, going to the apple farm, enjoying summers in Bear Mountain, and having adventures in the woods near my parents' summer home in North Carolina. Daniel made my life adventurous and we always created fun together.

Who knew life would end sooner than expected? In August of 1991, my 16-year-old brother Daniel Tyrone Taylor was murdered two weeks after my 14th birthday. The grief, anger, denial, great sadness, and guilt that my brother's death caused me created great pain and confusion.

When Daniel was alive, our favorite activity was to talk about the future and what we would do when we got older. A recurring theme was that we would take our families together to Disney World. We fantasized about getting a hotel on the beach and enjoying the theme parks. Daniel never had an opportunity to go to Disney World. In 1992, my parents sent me there with a close family friend and her son. During my trip, I bought a blue Mickey Mouse button for my brother. When I returned home to The Bronx, I decided that the button would lie on my brother's headstone. However, it took a while to have the opportunity to place the button on the headstone because my brother was buried in North Carolina.

The opportunity finally arose for me to take the button. I waited for my family members to leave me alone with Daniel; and when that opportunity came, I said to him, "Daniel, if you forgive me, when I come back, this button will be here." That same night, a tornado came through the area; I panicked and needed to check on the button. I had not secured the button, so any wind could have moved it. My parents said that we could not go back; we had to go home. It took a year to get back to the gravesite and, amazingly, the button was still there, although faded. The moment I saw the button, I had a feeling of release, joy, and forgiveness. I knew that my brother's spirit protected the button, just as I knew that he would have protected me in high school, no matter what he said.

10 Ways to Get Grief Out and Healing In

By Ruby L. Taylor, M.S.W.

Through my personal experiences with grief and loss over the years, I have learned that in order to heal we must get our emotions out. It took me more than 15 years to grow through my brother's murder. It took me so long because I did not want to accept that he was dead, and instead of releasing my emotions, I kept everything inside of me and acted as though it did not matter. It is my hope that when you deal with grief and loss, you do it openly and honestly. Below, you will find steps to help you grow through any loss, no matter the circumstances. Accept the loss.

A loss can be due to death, divorce, imprisonment, and many more forms of disconnection. A loss is any separation or ending to someone or something valuable and loved.

1. Breathe.

2. Acknowledge grief as an individualized and different experience every time you face a loss.

3. Do not be afraid of grief.

4. Create a support circle of family and friends who can help you grow through your grief and loss.

5. Do not isolate yourself.

6. List 10 activities you enjoy doing and do them, one at a time.

7. Accept your feelings and remember that an emotion never stays the same or lasts forever.

8. Use writing or art to get your feelings out.

9. Create a memory box. Fill a box with pictures that remind you of the deceased, write favorite stories, draw pictures, add the deceased's favorite candy or any item that reminds you of your loss; and when you want to be close to him or her, look in the box.

10. Listen to music you love and dance, even if you are not a dancer.

Growing Through Hurt

By Nicki Higgins

I have experienced a lot of pain in the past: some with family, some with friends, and let's not even mention boyfriend relationships. I have been hurt numerous times by those I loved and trusted. My pain caused me to put up my guard and prepare for the next disappointment. It damaged me. I became extremely distant. I decided that the people who hurt me would become irrelevant. Whatever we shared as friends meant nothing to me. I became numb to their feelings; and before you knew it, in my mind, they no longer existed. Who deserves to be treated the way I was treated? No one! However, what about my feelings? Did I deserve what happened to me? No! Nonetheless, I don't deserve to carry it around in my heart, either.

I used to keep my feelings in. I did this to avoid an argument or tension between friends or family members. Now, I don't do that anymore. I express how I feel. How can I be fine if pain is still resting on my heart? I still carry it around in my mind and that's not healthy.

My old behavior not only caused stress, but it caused me not to be genuine, which is not my character. Therefore, today, I release this bad habit of holding onto negative feelings. I have a new habit of expressing how I feel and allowing myself to have peace by letting go of the pain.

Recently, I had a disagreement with a friend. Normally, we would argue and the tension would remain for days. However, this time, I didn't allow myself to prolong the situation. I gave it a day, so we could both calm down. The next day, we spoke as if nothing happened. I let it go! I was not going to have that dark cloud looming over my friendship.

We all make mistakes. I'm not a person who seeks revenge by hurting or retaliating. In the past, I would just become very distant and cold. Now, I just really and truly LET IT GO! Yes, it's still a process, but I'm willing to work at it. Through the grace of God, I am doing better. Letting go of the hurt and the pain from the past will allow me to see the beauty in what I have right now. Letting go has allowed me to trust again. Letting go has allowed me to love again. Letting go allowed me to see that there is sunshine after the rain. As a result, I'm more optimistic about life now than I have ever been, and it feels SO GOOD!

We are all beautiful in one way or another. Find what makes you feel beautiful and work with that. Is it your eyes or your smile? Maybe it's your legs or your personality. Whatever it is, use that beauty as a stepping stone to build your confidence.

My feet, my thighs, my lips, my eyes; I'm LOVING what I see!

—*India Arie, songwriter and musician*

Love yourself, because no one can do it better than you.

—*Ruby Taylor*

Priceless Action One:

HEALING

Life is filled with good, bad, and in-between experiences. We must be able to accept and grow through all experiences, especially the bad ones. Ignoring our hurt, anger, frustration, and disappointments will create major problems. We must face them head on. For example, if you just found out that you passed the gym class you thought you failed, that is a great moment of relief and celebration and you should rejoice in that moment. If two weeks later your boyfriend breaks up with you and your response is "nothing good ever happens in my life," you are making a generalization and need to put things into perspective. You forgot about passing gym class, and you were happy when you first started going out with your boyfriend because those were good experiences.

Now, you are facing a bad moment of betrayal and the end of your relationship. Deal with life a moment at a time. Even though you may feel as though your hurt will never end, remember that emotions never stay the same. In order to grow through the bad feelings, we must embrace them. You can grow through any circumstance if you are willing to face it and allow yourself to feel not so good in the beginning. Over time, you will feel better. How can you feel better? Create a healing arts journal.

Healing Arts Journal

Do you remember when you were a child how much you loved coloring, cutting, and gluing? Don't you miss that? The Healing Arts Journal is here to help you reclaim that inner-child artist and to increase your confidence for greatness at the same time. Art healing and journaling are not about the masterpiece or selling your work. This exercise is about healing; and in order to have high self-worth, we must heal our broken areas. Don't worry if you think you can't draw, paint, or write. The space in the journal is for your creative art healing. It does not have to be perfect; it just has to be done. No one needs to see your artwork. Write, draw, and color your thoughts and emotions out. When we acknowledge and express our hurt and pain, healing comes over time.

In the back of this book, you can begin your healing arts journal. Find a spiral notebook, blank paper, or unused binders, and/or use the computer to write and draw about life actions that hurt you in the past. Start today.

II

EDUCATIONAL STRUGGLES and VICTORIES

NOTES

STILL STRIVING

By Shanta Whitaker, Ph.D.

Dear Priceless,

I know life can be hard and may not always seem fair, but I want to encourage you ALWAYS to dream big because you never know what you may accomplish. As a young child and through high school, I wasn't very popular. I am not saying that I didn't have friends, but I definitely wasn't a "cool" kid. I was teased endlessly about being tall (imagine being 5'9 in middle school) and being light-skinned. The phrases "Jolly Green Giant" and "she thinks she is white" still haunt me slightly today. Instead of allowing my negative experiences to keep me down, I looked for and found my PRICELESS spirit and went onto graduate high school, Virginia Union University, and Yale University.

Coming from a single-parent home, I had to watch my mother struggle to make sure my sister and I had a roof over our heads. Although I appreciated all that my mother did, I wished for what many of my peers had. Their parents went to college and were still married. I sometimes wished that my family could have been like the Huxtables from the "Cosby Show," but it wasn't my reality. My mother had to work a lot. The responsibility of babysitting my sister often fell on me, and I could not participate in many school activities. I felt very sad and alone most of the time, but I also began to use my imagination and dream of what I wanted the rest of my life to look like.

Because my mother dropped out of college, she held up her life as an example of what she did not want me to follow. She drove me to focus on education so that I would not be dependent on anyone and because that is something that nobody can take away. Although I did not really appreciate the value of an education when I was younger, I still dedicated myself to my work as my mother suggested. My favorite preacher, Dr. Powell, probably says it best: "Work now so that you can play later." Yes, everyone around you may seem as though they are having a ball while you are focusing on your academics, but I urge you to look at those same people 10 years from now. I guarantee you that if you focus on your education now, you will have fun later, while they are paying for not working on education.

Eventually, I began to fall in love with science; I wanted to be a doctor so that I could help underserved minorities and women. The first step on that journey was going to college, and because I did so well academically in high school, I was able to get a scholarship to attend Virginia Union University.

Attending a historically black college was a wonderful experience. Priceless, I assure you that you may feel unpopular now, but it will change in college. You will be exposed to a wide variety of people with the common goal of pursuing education. I can almost guarantee that there will be people in school with whom you will identify. College helped me finally spread my wings and I made many friends. I stopped feeling insecure about my height and complexion because there were plenty of people who looked like me.

I also had the opportunity to make up for all of the high school activities I missed. College gave me the chance to join many great organizations, and I even pledged a sorority.

The educational desire that my mother instilled in me, did not go away. I continued to focus on my education and explored the medical field. However, by my sophomore year, I was aware that medicine was not for me; I couldn't deal with losing my patients or the smell of human blood.

Thanks to my college adviser, Dr. Madu, and a class I took that same year, I was able to find a new passion in microbiology, and I decided to become a microbiologist. Microbiologists study microscopic organisms, such as bacteria, viruses, and protozoa and the diseases that are caused by them. Although my mother and some of my friends couldn't understand why I deviated from wanting to be a physician, they supported my dreams. Because of their faith in me and my growing self-confidence, I had the courage to apply to several top schools for Ph.D. programs in microbiology. In the end, I was accepted to Yale University's Ph.D. program; and six years later, I now hold a Ph.D. in microbiology. I am the first in my family to receive a Ph.D. and the first to attend an Ivy League institution.

Priceless, I believe that everyone should have someone in her life who inspires her and believes in her, even when she doesn't believe in herself. My supporters were my mother, Dr. Madu, and a large group of friends. Maybe you don't get that encouragement from your family, but it doesn't mean that you can't find it elsewhere. Maybe it's your mentor, an aunt, a teacher, a friend, or even a person who you will meet on the street. If you still can't find that support, then it is my wish that you find the strength to be able to encourage yourself and it is my hope that eventually you are led to supportive people. You are priceless and you deserve to have priceless support around you.

I wrote the following poem when I was around 9 or 10, and it represents how I feel about my life. I hope it will inspire you as much as it is still inspiring me.

When I was born, my climb began,
Up that steep hill.
I climb step by step,
Up that steep hill,
Facing many challenges.
As I grow older, I will
Still climb the hill,
Letting no one stop me.
I will not give up.
Still climbing,
I will face hurdles,
Doing my best to reach the top,
Strong enough to withstand the trials,
Still trudging, I will climb
This steep, jagged hill,
Climbing 'til I reach
What no one else has seen.

Dr. Shanta Whitaker's Yale
University Graduation

Priceless Action Two:

CIRCLE OF TRUST

In the movie *Meet the Fockers*, Mr. Focker talks about the circle of trust. I love that philosophy. The circle of trust is the creation of a small group of friends and family who you love, respect and have loyalty to, and they do the same for you. Your circle of trust supports you and celebrates who you are in all stages of your life, and you do the same for them. Working as a school social worker in an urban high school recently, I watched a group of 12th grade girls develop into young women. One girl in the group was failing, and her friend stated, "I will do all I can to help you pass." The other student wanted to drop out of school, but her friend convinced her to stay in school. In June 2011, I watched proudly as they both received their diplomas.

When you have a circle of trust, they will support and encourage you. Beware of those who do not respect you or your values and discourage you from doing what makes you happy and successful. If you do not have a circle of trust, you can create one over time.

Who is in your circle of trust? Sometimes people in your circle will take up more than one role and that is okay. Some people may have one person to fill all of the roles, while others may have two people and some may have five people to fill the roles. Everyone is different and that is okay!

THE ROLES IN YOUR CIRCLE OF TRUST

a. Who can you make you laugh?

b. Who will listen to you whenever you need to talk?

c. Who makes you feel loved?

d. Who will listen to you without judgment?

e. Who will give you words of encouragement and hope?

f. Who will let you cry without interruption?

g. With whom can you have a great time?

h. Who will give you a push when needed?

MY EDUCATION IS PRICELESS

By Sylvia Morris

The year I was in the eighth grade shaped my "priceless" thinking. At the end of the school year, I had a sense of worthiness and enough self-esteem to carry me through my life. I grew up in the era of sharecropping, which is a way of farming. A family lives on the farm of the landowner and the family plants, cares for, and harvests the crops, paying for all the expenses incurred. At the end of the harvest, the profits are supposedly divided equally. Generally, the landowner was the only one to keep a record of all expenses and you had to take the landowner's word for the records that were kept. Until that time, sharecropping was the major source of income for the people in my small town of Windsor, N.C. By the time I reached eighth grade, things were changing as people got jobs in factories and left the farm. That's when I realized that I was considered to be low class. It was around that same time when reality hit me in the face and showed me just how poor I was.

In school, the children of preachers and teachers had the highest status. Next were the children whose parents brought home a paycheck every week. If you had light skin, you were looked upon favorably. The lowest on the totem pole were the children of sharecroppers. However, I refused to stay on the bottom. My parents instilled in me the idea that I was just as good as anybody else, so I decided that even though I came from a sharecropping family and my skin was not light, that I would just have to be smarter than anybody in my class.

Every year, students were required to take a state achievement test. Imagine how I felt when the scores were posted and my name appeared on the top of the list. Yes, the daughter of a sharecropper made the highest score in the county. My achievement didn't stop there. At eighth grade graduation, my name appeared in the program as the valedictorian. It was priceless! Education is priceless. No matter what your social status is, **YOU ARE PRICELESS!**

Priceless Action Three

ACKNOWLEDGE YOUR LIFE VALUES

Take a moment and think about what you value. What is important to you? Examples: spiritual connection, love of family, creativity, education, communication, learning, helping others, career, relationships, personal growth, new adventures, and/or academic achievement.

LIST YOUR TOP FIVE VALUES

1.

2.

3.

4.

5.

Understanding your values will help you to make decisions based upon what is important to you and what you value. Knowing your values is critical in increasing inner value and self-acceptance. Understanding your value will also help you when Facebook or other social drama occurs. How? I am glad you asked. If it is not something you value, is it really something you should fight for or put energy into?

For example, you value education so that you can reach your career goals. An ex-friend on Facebook curses at you and makes up lies about you and your boyfriend on Facebook. Your friends say that you should punch her in her face, and you know you will be suspended and may even be kicked out of school if you fight. You must remember education is what you value and your ex-friend really does not matter in the bigger picture. Instead of fighting, talk it out. Try to find a mediator, a peer, or an adult in your school so that you can say what's in your heart and find a solution to the problem.

Go after what is really important to you, and your self-worth will increase one step at a time. Remember, every decision you make should be based upon your values.

"*LIFE FOR ME AIN'T BEEN NO CRYSTAL STAIR.*"

Lucinda Lumpkin

In a world that increasingly prides itself on external appearances, young women from all types of cultures desire to be beautiful and smart based on the social standards of the time. Many of us spend our whole lives buying the right clothes, having the perfect haircut, exercising, dieting, and putting on make-up, simply spending endless hours and lots of money trying to feel good about ourselves, but never measuring up to the many airbrushed or otherwise enhanced images portrayed to us in movies, TV, and in fashion magazines. After all that expended energy and money, we are usually left feeling rejected, dejected, and with little self-worth.

It seems like only yesterday when I was that young girl who didn't know how valuable she really was. That famous line from Langston Hughes' poem "Life for me ain't been no crystal stair" was certainly true of my life. From the very beginning, I experienced failure at school; and as a result of low self-esteem, throughout my teens I simply didn't like myself. I felt worthless.

My kindergarten teacher suggested to my mother that I repeat kindergarten. My mother, being the advocate she was, would not hear of it. "Kids don't fail kindergarten," she said. "Besides, she knows her ABCs, she can count to at least one hundred, she writes legibly, and she knows all her identity information." It was settled; I was moved along to the first grade. Though I remember little about my initial year in that grade, one occasion stands out. While waiting for a conference with my teacher, my mother looked around the classroom and saw a bulletin board featuring various words focusing on vowel sounds. She asked me whether I knew the sounds. "A, E, I, O, U, and sometimes Y," I said. "Yes". "What are their sounds?" she asked. She might as well have been speaking in a foreign language. I couldn't answer her question and she seemed disappointed in me. "You should know that, Cindy," she said, before going over each vowel sound with me.

I ended up repeating the first grade, but I don't recall much more. I do remember my second year in the first grade. I did very well and made the honor roll the entire year. My mother was very proud of me. "I knew my baby could do it," she said. I moved on to the second grade on my own merit; but then a new problem arose, or perhaps the same problem had just been hiding, biding its time. Suddenly, failure in school once again became a major part of my life. When I was pushed on to the third grade, school became more and more difficult for me. It was extremely frustrating.

My third grade teacher was kind; instead of failing me, she placed me in the fourth grade. My report card literally read, "Placed in the fourth grade." Just as when I was in kindergarten, I realized that the word "placed" meant that I hadn't earned the right to be in fourth grade on my own. I spent that summer with a private tutor.

I'm not sure how much it helped, but I understood by then that academics just did not make much sense to me.

Thus, my journey to overcome a learning disability and reclaim my self-worth began in the fourth grade. It was then that I was referred to a special-education program. For many years, I thought this strategy did more harm than good. It was a long time before I realized that the very program that had contributed to my low self-esteem and lack of confidence was, in part, the program that saved my life.

Life in middle school is an emotional roller coaster, and this already taxing phase is further complicated for a special-education student by realizing the difference between oneself and one's regular-education peers. This was a most traumatic point in my academic career, a turbulent period during which my peers began wondering why they only saw me at physical education class and why I, a sixth grader, had lunch with the eighth grade students. It was also at this point that I began to feel the embarrassment that usually comes along with being labeled "special."

However, high school marked a fresh start in my education and my life. I was more outspoken, confident, and ready to put the unpleasant scholastic experiences of the past behind me. Having endured the special-education program, I made a complete turnaround. My self-esteem and confidence shot through the roof, and I began to make significant academic progress. Many of my fellow students had forgotten, or seemed not to care anymore, that I had ever been in special education. They now saw me as a leader; and as a result, I started seeing myself as one. I became increasingly involved in extracurricular activities and held office in many of the organizations in which I was a member.

I experienced a tremendous transformation during high school. Not even the negative situations could set me back. I was determined to be something bigger and better. Just when I thought things couldn't get any better, I learned that my essay had been chosen over many other honor students' papers, and I was one of two student speakers at graduation! When I sat down to write that speech, I wanted to express gratitude to my mother and to Mrs. Bly, Mrs. Jones, and Mrs. Tucker, those special-education teachers who worked so hard to help me learn.

I knew that it was their dedication, love, and support that had enabled me to reach the point of being able to manage my disability. I was still, however, unable to admit who I was. The pain, shame, and embarrassment were too fresh for me to relive, so I expressed as much as I could without giving anything away, including not naming those who had the greatest and most positive impact on me. As my family, friends, and teachers looked on, I spoke articulately:

As a result of the academic failures, I felt that people looked down upon me. In turn, I looked down on myself. No matter how many good grades I made, in the end, I still felt worthless. However, years later, I know that feeling had less to do with my past failures and more to do with the fact that I didn't know who I was or how to take comfort and strength from my religion.

How do you determine the value of a thing? Is it determined by how it looks? No! The value of anything is determined by how much someone will pay for it. An example of this is in artwork, such as sculptures and paintings. I have seen some pretty weird sculptures and paintings. Some have seemed downright hideous. Some looked so bad to me that even if they cost $1, I would not have bought them. Lucky for the artist that the work's value is not determined by how it looks to me. Its value is determined by how much someone is willing to pay for it. There are collectors who are willing to pay some very big bucks for art because, even when I may not see the value in it, they do.

Similarly, your value does not come from any negative life experiences. Instead, it comes from how much you or others feel you are WORTH. Sister, just know this: You are WORTHY of ALL good things. You are the most valuable entity in this world. You Are Priceless!

Cindy Lumpkin is a mother, motivational speaker and author. She wrote Destined for Success, where she shares her journey of being labeled an individual with a learning disability and overcoming low self-esteem issues to becoming the successful goal-oriented individual that she is today. She is currently working on In Search of True Beauty, a book that helps young women and girls define beauty from a biblical perspective. Connect with Cindy Lumpkin on Facebook.

Lucinda Lumpkin's Wedding

Priceless Action Four

APPRECIATE FAILURES

In order to grow and to love ourselves, we must be OK with failure. We are not perfect; and at times, we will make wrong decisions. When I was in the 11th grade, I wanted to get my permit so that I could learn to drive. Therefore, my father took me and two of my siblings to the Department of Motor Vehicles to take the test. I was so excited and knew all I needed to use was my common sense to pass the test, even though my brother told me that I needed to read the book and study. When I took the test, I failed miserably.

Right after that failure, I studied to learn the various traffic signs and other laws of the road. Through my failure, I learned that I did not know what I needed to pass. I learned everything I could through reading the drivers' permit book and asking questions. Eventually, I passed and that was such a great moment in my life. It allowed me to be one step closer to driving. Even in our failures, we are lovable and worthy of success.

When you fail, please celebrate your effort and willingness to at least TRY. You are a winner when you try, fail, and learn. Often, success cannot come without failure. Determine what went wrong and how you can do better next time. It's OK to fail. Write down two failures and what you learned from them. Every failure brings us one step closer to SUCCESS.

1.

2.

NOTES

III

RELATIONSHIP STRUGGLES AND TRUIMPH

No Matter What

LORRAINE SELLARS

Regardless of where you began or how you got to where you are now, you have the power within to change. Every life is priceless, and no one else can steal your chosen destiny. I was never the smartest, the prettiest, the most popular, or the leader of the pack, but God has shown me how he uses ordinary people like me to do extraordinary things. As a teenager, I wanted to be part of the "in" crowd, and was looking for love in all the wrong places and never finding it. I managed to get accepted into a four-year college in spite of my high school counselor's advice that I should work and not go to college.

Although I progressed through my college years, a major change occurred during my senior year. During this last year of college, I became pregnant and the words from some of my family and friends were very hurtful. I struggled that last year, but I was determined to prove everybody wrong who spoke negative and ugly things about me and who predicted a limited future for me. With God's help and my willingness to trust him, I delivered my baby in

April, graduated with my class in May, and got a job in my field in June.

None of us can choose what type of environment we're born into, and sometimes we lack the power to fight through our circumstances early in life. If you learn to first love yourself and let the negative talk be your fuel to keep you moving forward, your outcome will hold great promise. Your actions alone can and will close the mouths of naysayers. We all make bad choices sometimes in life, but every experience is a stepping stone toward maturity, and every girl's life can have a priceless story to tell. Do not allow anyone state that you can never change or be something great. You are priceless!

Lorraine Sellars

Priceless Action Five

LOCATE YOUR RICHES

We can all point out our weaknesses but rarely consider our strengths. Take a moment to think about the riches you have within you. I know a young woman who had a very difficult family life. She was sexually abused by several family members, mistreated by her foster family, and rejected by her biological family. Regardless of what trials life brought her, she had a great personality, was friendly and sweet every time I saw her. Just seeing her made me smile. Her riches are her personality and inner strength, and this young woman's riches enriched my life.

How do you make your life rich and make the lives of others around you richer? Find at least five to 10 things you admire about yourself related to your personality or abilities. For example, maybe you can make people laugh; you're sensitive to others' feelings; you are driven; resourceful; articulate; good with children; a natural in math; or have a caring heart for others. Write these riches down and read the list whenever you feel your priceless value going down.

LIST YOUR RICHES

1.

2.

3.

4.

5.

Does He Know His Own Worth?

CHELSA BROWN

We make a note to tell our girls, "You're beautiful. You're smart. YOU'RE WORTH IT!" But lately I've asked myself, how often are our boys told this? This thought crossed my mind after having a conversation with a male friend who doesn't really know what it's like to date what he defines as "a real woman," a woman who knows her self-worth. We often wonder why some men and boys treat women and girls the way that they do. Have we ever stopped to wonder, "Why do they think so negatively about females?" Society has accepted that men will be men and boys will be boys. They're tough, strong, and have these big male egos.

We sometimes forget to help nurture boys so that they know they, too, have worth and should have the best.

There's this double standard that we all are aware of. Males often sleep with whomever, whenever, and however. People say, "It doesn't affect them the way it does girls." I beg to differ! Think about it. What does this man or boy think of himself that he is willing to give himself to so many different women or girls?

If a female is in the company of someone who doesn't think much of himself, how can she possibly think much of herself? Does he feel and know he is worth it? Has he ever been told that? Who took him under his wing and said, "You deserve the best?" If he doesn't know his own worth, how can we expect him to know the worth of a young lady and treat her as such? My point is that it is IMPERATIVE that you know YOUR WORTH! Know your worth so that you can recognize if a young man, who may be interested in you, knows his own worth. If he doesn't know that he deserves the best, he won't know what the best is when it's staring him in the face. The best is YOU! You Are Priceless!

I Am Love

Najair Williams

I have a heart.
I wonder when people will get along.
I hear people screaming.
I see people dying.
I want people to stop fighting.
I am Love.
I pretend that this is a happy world.
I touch the hearts of people who feel empty.
I feel as though I have no meaning.
I worry that this world will never heal.
I cry about all the lives being lost.
I am Love.
I understand that people need help.
I say that someday there will be no wars.
I dream about happiness.
I try to heal the broken hearts.
I hope that one day people will realize
I am Love.

Priceless Action Six

Smile

Smile. Smiling helps us feel better. Research has proven that smiling transforms our brain and automatically puts us in a positive state of mind. How often have you heard people make excuses such as, "My mother treats my brother better than she treats me. I have nothing to smile about. I don't have hip clothes and sometimes people make fun of me. My father always breaks his promises; I have nothing to smile about. I am failing four of my classes; what do I have to smile about?"

Everyone has experienced moments that have caused pain, shame, frustration, anger, or hurt. Still, I say, "SMILE." (Think of one or more things that can make you smile; write down a moment that made you smile. It can be from your personal life, a TV show, movies, or something you observed or said. If you cannot find anything to smile about today, think about something from the past). Smiling gives you huge benefits. Your smile will help you feel better and also help others. According to Dr. Mark Stibich, a researcher who specializes in creating efficient solutions for public health problems, smiling:

1. Boosts the immune system

2. Increases positive affect

3. Reduces stress

4. Lowers blood pressure

5. Enhances other people's perception of you (makes you

   more attractive to them)

Have you smiled lately? SMILE NOW! Close your eyes and put yourself in the moment you just wrote about. Let your mouth turn upward in a grin while your feeling of stress lessens and well-being increases.

Notes

IV

FAMILY ISSUES

NOTES

A Woman's Worth

Ruby Y. Burke

My Childhood

Growing up in the Washington, D.C., metropolitan area, I had a normal childhood. I guess it was as normal as any childhood. My parents divorced when I was only 3 years old. It is not a surprise considering my mother got pregnant to trap my father. Once she got him, she decided he was not good enough. My father was in the military; and when he was discharged, he came to the Washington area. His intention of returning to South Carolina to marry the mother of his child and to raise his already-existing son changed because another woman, my mother, had different plans for him. All she saw were dollar signs. My mother already had my brother and really wanted someone to take care of her.

She thought that the only way she could get that security was to have another baby, and that is when my unsuspecting father got trapped. My father was the oldest of 16 children. He helped his mother raise his siblings, and he didn't get a chance to finish school. While home in South Carolina, my father met a young woman and she became pregnant. Back then, joining the military was the way to succeed; and since he didn't have an education, he felt that was what he needed to do to take care of his son and his son's mother.

Unfortunately, he met my mother and she became pregnant with me. Because of the love he had for her, he married her. In order to make a living after the military, he started working in construction. Construction is a dirty job, and my mother, who had nothing, could not be with someone who had a dirty job. Therefore, she sought pleasure outside of the marriage. As you can guess, the end result was not good for my father. That affair produced a child, and my father raised my sister as though she were his own; he did the same things for her that he did for me.

After a short time, my parents got a divorce. It was the best thing for all of us because I witnessed the arguments and all of the anger that my father had inside. Even though he still loved my mother very much, he was angry at her for what she had done to the family he so desperately wanted to have. After the divorce, my father became very distant and was not an affectionate man. He did not hug us, and I have never heard him say, "I love you." His way to show love was to buy us everything we wanted. Sadly, he has carried these hurt feelings with him for the past 40-plus years. He has had other relationships, but he feels as though women are nothing, that all women are like my mother and that men should watch out for them.

Unfortunately, when my sister was about 12 years old, my mother sent her to live with my father. At the time, we did not know that he was not her biological father. He paid for her to go to private school, just as he did for me, but he was verbally abusive. He took out his hatred of women on her. In turn, she grew to despise him and his woman-hating attitude.

As I got older and men started paying more attention to me, I looked for the affection that I was not getting at home. I was a darker skinned child and back in the day, boys and men seemed to favor lighter skinned girls/women. So there were several obstacles in my path early on.

Teenage Mother

When I was 16, I got pregnant. My mother decided that since I was grown enough to get pregnant and I didn't want to get married, then I was grown enough to move out on my own. So, my sister and I got a house. I went to a private school and everyone was surprised that I continued to go to school. The nuns were angry and wanted me to quit. They said that it was not Christian to be single and pregnant. Well, I knew I needed my education more now than ever.

I managed with the help of my father. I had my son when I was 17, and it was just the two of us for many years.

I loved to date. Still not recognizing my self-worth, I dated all kinds of men and was willing to do whatever I needed to do to keep them with me. Most of the time, they were not asking; I was just giving because I thought that is what I had to do.

Young Adulthood

As an adult, my skin complexion had not changed but my features had. I was considered beautiful, but I did not realize that I had become a beautiful young woman. Even though I was told how beautiful I was, I still could not see it. All I saw was a dark-skinned little girl that people had made fun of. It was never instilled in me that I was beautiful and that the color of my skin did not change that.

I am now the co-founder and director of East Coast operations for a nonprofit organization Sisters in Harmony (www.sistersinharmonystore.com). We are working to restore positive images of women. We know this starts with our children, and that is why we mentor and have workshops to promote the positive works of our youth.

Priceless Action Seven

PUSH

We must acknowledge life's dark days, embrace them and *push* our way through them. We will not always have great times, but we must not allow negative experiences to stop our progress or make us miserable. Over the years, I have made many wrong decisions, and they have helped me to be successful in life. One bad decision was cutting school because it caused me to fail. When I began high school, I rarely attended classes. I would hang out around the school, take a train ride with my friends, or enjoy a party at someone's house. When my parents questioned me about the letters and phone calls from school, I lied and said I was late and the school made a mistake and marked me absent. My mother always said the same thing: "It is going to catch up with you."

I believed that my mother did not know what she was talking about. How wrong I was! During my high school years, every summer I was forced to go to summer school, and even in my senior year, I came up short. New York City public schools offered night school for students who needed to makeup credits. In order for me to graduate with my class, I had to go to regular school from 7:45 a.m. to 2:45 p.m. and night school from 4:45 to 9:45 p.m.

Instead of just giving up and skipping school, I finally took responsibility and found out that missing school was my problem and attending school would solve it. The crucial turning point was when I found a new group of friends. If I continued with my previous friends and never pushed myself, I would never have graduated high school. By *pushing* through my anger, frustration, irritation, and nagging parents, I was able to graduate, to enjoy senior prom, senior pictures, and the famous senior trip to Virginia Beach, Va.

In the end, I learned to be careful with my friends and my decisions. My senior year was very difficult and I often wanted to give up, but I *pushed* my way through. When struggles come along and life does not go as planned, please remember that you can push through it.

Even when you do not feel like getting out of bed, push on. If there is a time when you don't feel that you can be nice to yourself or others, push on until you find a way to succeed.

Notes

V

LIFE LESSONS

NOTES

Important Lessons

Tina Martin

Over the years, in dealing with people during the challenges of their lives and some notable challenges of my own, *I have learned to respect other people's boundaries and to make them feel safe.* I understand that most of what people project is a reflection of themselves and not of me. They could be angry, hurt, self-loathing, or uninspired, yet most will attempt to project that feeling onto others. Misery loves company. When you meet these people and they try to make you feel less than a full person or less than a success, you need to understand that how they feel is not your fault. Don't listen to people who just want to put you down (which they do oftentimes to make themselves feel or look better).Instead, DO listen to advice from those you KNOW love you and want you TO SUCCEED.

Life is precious, so *reach out and make a difference in someone's life*. It could change your own. Understand that it is very difficult for people who are hurting or in need to ask for help. At such times, it is up to you to offer help. You may need to provide a much-needed shoulder to lean on or friendship to trust in. That could make all the difference in the world in helping someone to face the challenges he or she is facing.

Don't settle for anything less than what makes you happy and makes you shine. We are in charge of our lives and the decisions we make. Bad things do happen to good people; we just need to know we have everything in us to survive and be better.

Each year of your life is like a movie; some are dramas, while others are action-packed. However, the best ones are the success stories. *You need to understand what your strengths are and make sure you complete things to the best of your ability.* Don't sit in the audience watching life play out. Instead, be a part of the moment and make something good happen. Five years from now, you won't remember the day-to-day struggle, only the highlight reel. In the end, you can look back on the success you produced and be proud.

SMILE, people are more receptive and friendly when you SMILE.

I find music helpful to get through a challenge. Here is my suggested play list:

"*Tapestry*" by Carole King

"*Friends*" "*From a Distance*" and "*The Rose*" by Bette Midler

"*I Believe in You*" and "*Untold Stories*" by Sinead O'Connor

"*One Moment in Time*" by Whitney Houston

"*Video*" by India Arie

"*Don't Know Why*" by Norah Jones

"*In My Life*" by Allison Crouse

"*I'm Every Woman*" by Chaka Khan

"*The Voice Within*" by Annekei

"*The Glory of Love*" by Kathy Troccoli

"*You've Got a Friend*" by Mina Tank

"*Beautiful*" by Christina Aguilera

"*Big Girls Don't Cry*" by Fergie

"*Breakaway*" by Lemonade Mouth

"*Chasing Pavements*" by Adele

"*I am Woman*" by Helen Reddy

"*Don't Rain On My Parade*" by Barbra Streisand

"*Independent Woman*" by Flyzee

"*Keep Holding On*" by Avril Lavigne

"*A New Day Has Come*" by Celine Dion

"*That Don't Impress Me Much*" and "*Man! I Feel Like a Woman!*"
    by Shania Twain

"*Strong Enough*" by Cher

"*These Are the Days*" by 10,000 Maniacs

"*True Colors*" by Cyndi Lauper

"*I've Got a Life*" by Eurythmics

"*Survivor*" by The American Mall Cast

"*All Fired Up*" and "*Hit Me with Your Best Shot*" by Pat Benatar

"*Ray of Light*" by Madonna

"*Get the Party Started*," "*So What*" and "*Perfect*" by Pink

"*Miss Independent*" by Kelly Clarkson

"*Stand in the Rain*" by Superchick

"*Firework*" by Katy Perry

"*Breakthrough*" by Lemonade Mouth

"*Born This Way*" by Lady Gaga

Priceless Action Eight

VOLUNTEER

We must learn ways to give back. Find an activity you enjoy and do it. At times, we must stop focusing on self only and lend a helping hand to our fellow women or men. Find an organization, school, family, or community member to whom you can be a blessing. You do not need money or a lot of time to volunteer. Find the experience that works for you. Doing good things for others empowers our inner being to feel worthy and satisfied. When we help others, our inner value goes up, and we feel good about ourselves. Go out and help someone else.

Here are some great organizations to consider volunteering for:
- Do Something http://www.dosomething.org/volunteer
- Glamour Gals http://glamourgals.org
- United Nations Girls' Education Initiative http://www.ungei.org/
- Girls Inc. http://www.girlsinc.org
- AllyKatzz http://www.allykatzz.com
- United Way http://liveunited.org

RUBY L. TAYLOR

NOTES

VI

SELF-WORTH

New Mirror

Beth Humpert and Birthe Kleischmann

Many of us struggle with negative patterns of thinking. Before real, permanent change takes place, we must change in the way we perceive ourselves.

My friend, Birthe Kleischmann, who lives in Denmark, has developed an exercise called Old Mirror, New Mirror. For years, she and her husband served as missionaries in Lesotho, Africa. Now, she is a licensed family therapist, and since we are friends, she has given me some informal therapy when I need help, via on-line chatting.

Birthe introduced me to a concept that she uses to help people make solid changes in their lives. The following is Birthe's explanation.

"The Old Mirror mostly consists of negative words. We could have picked them up during our youth, when hearing words spoken to or about us by others. For example, an ex-boyfriend or ex-girlfriend, who broke up with you in anger, may have said hurtful words that stuck in your mind. For some strange reason, we tend to remember negative words much better than positive ones, thus letting these words become the truth about ourselves, our negative self-image.

"Write down all of the negative words that pop into your head. Once you have written the negative words in The Old Mirror and you have acknowledged that this mirror is not healthy to keep looking into, you are ready to look at your New Mirror.

"In order to fill in positive words in your New Mirror, start listening for positive words about yourself from family, friends, or teachers. Pick them up, much like picking pretty flowers and putting them in a vase. Write them in your New Mirror.

"You may find it hard, at the beginning, to believe these positive words about yourself because you are so used to hearing and remembering the negative words, repeating them over and over in your mind. Believe the positive words and feed on them, incorporating them into your way of thinking about yourself.

Look into your New Mirror on a daily basis and you will notice how you begin to like what you see. You may want to place a drawing you make of your old self in your room, where you can't help but look at it every day."

"How do I view myself in this old mirror?" These are some of the things I wrote down to answer to that question.

Old Mirror – Words in the Mirror

Rejected: Rejection means insecurity. Synonyms: inadequate, unacceptable, lacking in qualities others possess.

Envious: Covet others' qualities; constant judgment and comparison with others.

Unpleasant: Miserable, loner.

Needy: Looking for continual approval; co-dependent versus interdependent.

Tomboyish: Uncomfortable expressing my femininity.

Fat: Food was my comfort; overeating covered insecurity.

Hardened: Defensive and fearful; emotionally distant in relationships.

Next, begin to ask about your new mirror, starting with, "What does my new mirror look like?" Draw this new image on a piece of paper.

My new mirror was oval with a natural wood frame. "What kind of wood," I asked? It has unusual wood, like that used by wood-carvers, with lots of marks that make it unique. I then realized and wrote these thoughts, "Knots and other imperfections seem undesirable to many people, but those who appreciate God's creation and one-of-a-kind beauty like them. I don't need to care about the opinion of others because, in God's eyes, I am beautifully made."

Ask yourself about the words that go along with your new mirror, "How do I see myself in this new mirror?" Following are some of the answers I heard.

New Mirror – Words in the Mirror

1. Big eyes: visionary, intuitive, perceptive

2. Big-hearted: compassionate

3. Beloved: well loved

4. Satisfied: not lacking any good thing in life

5. Acceptable and accepted

6. Beautiful, pretty

7. Empathetic: warm, nurturing

There is more to my story of transformation, but the mirror concept is a powerful tool. Events, words, and actions combined to form those old images of words from the past. New positive events, words, and actions have gradually uprooted the old and reshaped my self-image, which is much more positive (and worthy).

If you find yourself stuck in thinking, go and take a look at the drawing of your old mirror. You will recognize some of the words and feelings that entangle you. Turn from that old way in your heart and flip the page over to your new mirror. Ponder the words that describe the way God created you: *unique* and *priceless*. Take them in as much as you can and be transformed, moment-by-moment, into that new creation, that wholesome YOU.

Priceless Action Nine

EMBRACE THE HIGHER POWER

In order to know your real self and embrace your value, you must respect and acknowledge the bigger power in the universe. Yes, I am referring to the one who created you, and no, I am not referring to your parents. I am referring to LOVE/GOD. Creating a relationship, a personal relationship, with your creator is the first step in understanding, celebrating, and acknowledging your self-worth. God loved you so much and knew you were worthy since the beginning. He made the decision to create YOU!

A MAN'S POINT OF VIEW

By Shawn Kwadena Brown

When I was first asked to participate in this project, I thought to myself, "Man, what a huge honor," but at the same time, "Man, what am I going to say?" But shortly after, I began to ponder a bit and two women came to mind: my mother and my wife, two of the strongest women I know.

Both have been hurt in one way or another. Through resilience and strength, they remembered their value. They have evolved into truly virtuous women.

If there was one thing I could say to you, young Queen, it would be to remember your value. You are more precious than you realize.

I regard my mother (Pat) and my wife (Dayla) as two of the strongest women I know because they did not allow their circumstances to dictate their value to them. For my mother, becoming pregnant at the age of 16 in the early 70's (with me), and deciding to keep the baby regardless of what that meant for her future, showed an impeccable amount of courage. She endured embarrassment, ridicule, abandonment, and sometimes, physical abuse. She could have chosen to abort. Because of her choice, I write to you as someone who has been eternally blessed my entire life. She did not marry my biological father (who I met when I was 12 and with whom I have a growing relationship today). Instead, she has been married to my stepfather for nearly 40 years.

My wife Dayla was a girl from the South Bronx, who endured the issues of growing up without a father for the first nine years of her life. With the help of her mother and eventually her stepfather, she worked hard to stay off the streets of the city. She was able to go from the Bronx to Brown University, an Ivy League school. Again, both women never forgot their value. They did not allow their circumstances to dictate who they were or how far they could go.

While I have your attention, please allow me to add that no one person is worth losing yourself. Therefore, when you find yourself in a relationship with a guy and you begin to wonder what he truly feels for you, don't! I see too many sisters, young and seasoned, doing all kinds of tricks and maneuvers to evaluate the man they're with, to get him to the place they want him to be or to find out what's taking so long for the proposal. The truth is, you don't and shouldn't have to do that. If a guy is really into you, he'll go through hoops to let you know when he is ready. If you don't feel it after a couple of months, he's just not that into you and might simply stick around for the benefits of your company . You don't want a guy like that because he'll be like that with everything. So, once again, I challenge you, young sisters, to remember your worth. You are worth more than gold. You are Priceless!

Priceless Action Ten

CHEER FOR YOURSELF

Cheerleaders cheer loudly and proudly for their team, letting them know they can do it. They cheer when they are winning or losing. The best cheerleader you have on your team is yourself. At times, our thoughts and words can be negative toward ourselves. Being harsh or critical is not good. Instead, be good to yourself and cheer through good and bad moments.

How and when should we cheer? Here is an example from my life. When I was in high school, I had a U.S. Government Regents test I had to pass to graduate. The morning of the test, my oldest sister told me she hoped that I failed. Walking to school with those words in my mind was really beginning to get to me. However, instead of allowing my sister's negativity to break me, I began to cheer for myself. I said "Ruby, you have got this test." I said that over and over. After the test, I knew I had passed with flying colors. No matter how much my sister's words bugged me, I allowed my cheer to be louder than the negative vibes.

A cheer does not have to have rhythm, but it *must* encourage and enforce an action. My cheer, aka self-talk, gave me the courage and inspiration to take the test with confidence. That was a great high school memory; just thinking about it makes me smile. Shutting up or ignoring someone who has sent hate your way is such a great moment. When we are second-guessing our actions, feeling as though we will fail, or feeling bad about what others are saying, we should use a cheer to go into action. When we do something great, I say also use a cheer to celebrate. Become a cheerleader for *you*.

In order to create a good cheer or self-talk, avoid generalizations; e.g., after making a mistake, don't say to yourself, "I can never get anything right." Instead, cheer yourself with kindness and encouragement and say, "I will get it right next time. Cheer yourself when you have failed. Make up a personal cheer for yourself, and when you are not feeling too great or mad at yourself, sing your cheer. Make up another cheer to celebrate your success; and when you do something good or great, sing your cheer. Go ahead; you deserve it! Cheer yourself on! My cheer is really simple and very effective: "Go, Ruby! Go, Ruby! Go, Ruby!"

Now is the time to create your own cheer.

CONCLUSION

Dear Priceless One,

I know life can be difficult and confusing, but I want to let you know you are PRICELESS, no matter what. Every step of the way, this book was written with YOU in mind. I was driven by the heart and voice of every young woman in the world, especially YOU.

We all have a story to tell, and in this book, you will find many great women sharing their obstacles and inspirations in the hope of inspiring you to reach your personal greatness. Life looks very different when you love yourself and have a high feeling of self-worth. Life is not easy, but I know it can be enjoyable, especially when you know your self-worth. When we love ourselves and get the pain, hurt, and anger out, we develop a peace within.

Remember life is not about reaching the greatness of your friend, sister, cousin, or Beyonce, Katy Perry, Oprah, President Obama, Bill Gates, Steve Jobs, or Selena Gomez. It is about reaching your own greatness, which will change our world for the better! We need you!

Are you ready to live with confidence and live like you are PRICELESS? I certainly hope your answer is YES!

Join me on this PRICELESS journey!

If you want to send us a comment or ask a question, email me, the author, Ruby Taylor at <u>Project@pricelessproject.com.</u>

VII

Notes, Inspiration, and Resources

Notes

INSPIRATIONAL QUOTES

All Quotes from Ruby L. Taylor, M.S.W.

Never allow your emotions to tell your attitude what to do. Keep a positive attitude, no matter what.

Changing the world begins with changing our words. What are you speaking into existence?

In order to change the world, first you must know that you are capable!

Set a goal. If you don't, you will never recognize your success. Ready. Set. Goal!

Smile. Someone needs to see your happiness!

Help young women problem-solve and you will help a generation reach its destiny!

Self-worth cannot be valued by the items we collect or wear; it can only be measured by the character and uniqueness we all possess.

Tell yourself that you are special, cute, gifted, and no one will ever compare to you. YOU ARE PRICELESS!

If you want to feel great about yourself, do something great for someone else. It really works. You are priceless!

When we use words that are positive, we open the door to our own healing. When we speak negatively, we open the door to our own destruction.

Whether you have reached your goal or not, you are still PRICELESS. Keep on reaching; and in time, you will be where you desire to be.

You are PRICELESS because no one will ever completely be able to take your place. Live like you are PRICELESS.

Opportunities never happen unless effort and faith are present. You are PRICELESS!

If you have a learning disability, smile. You are still PRICELESS!

Smile. God decided that you were worth creating and ensured that you are alive for this moment. You are PRICELESS!

I love helping a teenager turn tears into a smile. I love my career!

Never make a decision based upon emotions. You are PRICELESS, so take your time and make a wise decision.

This is a moment we will not ever get back, so make sure you make it a PRICELESS ONE because you are PRICELESS.

Events can make us forget our true self-worth. Just remember, no matter what, you are PRICELESS!

Patience is the difference between peace and hell. Have patience; your peace depends upon it. YOU ARE PRICELESS!

Take a day off from life and celebrate your existence!

Guidance

By Vanessa Van Petten

QUESTIONS

How can a young woman increase her self-worth?

When girls take leadership roles, their self-worth grows by leaps and bounds. There are many ways a girl can increase her self-worth by becoming a leader. Try to start small by organizing a family dinner or family project. This works especially well for younger girls. Take the reins for a family day and plan the activities, or make one meal per week. An important leadership principle is learning to plan and to organize people, so begin in your own family. See if you can take an art project and plan the details of buying supplies, getting everyone together and sticking to a goal.

You can also plan an event or party. Event planning, working with people and making something appealing is really important, especially if you want to be a leader with something to sell or promote, such as a cause or message. Plan a fundraiser at your school, organize a surprise party or family reunion. Do anything where you can exercise your planning skills and working with other people. Girls can also try to run for a student election at school or start a group or local club, which are great for self-worth and resumes.

ABOUT VANESSA VAN PETTEN

Vanessa Van Petten is one of the nation's youngest experts, or "youthologists," on parenting and adolescents. She wrote her first parenting book from the teen's perspective when she was 17. After winning the Mom's Choice Award in 2009, she launched her popular parenting blog, RadicalParenting.com, which she writes with 120 other teenage writers from ages 12 to 20 to answer questions from parents. Her approach of bringing parents and teens together, as well as adapting social and emotional intelligence for families, has been featured on CNN, CBS Miami, Fox New York and in The Wall Street Journal and Teen Vogue. She was also on *The Real Housewives of Orange County* helping the parents and teens. Her book *Do I Get My Allowance Before or After I'm Grounded?* was published in 2011. Link: http://www.radicalparenting.com

RUBY TAYLOR ANSWERS TEEN QUESTIONS

I really like this boy and he really likes me, too. The problem is he has a girlfriend. What should I do? Brianna

Hello, Priceless. One. You are worth a boyfriend who is NOT in a relationship. As a young lady, you should always respect someone else's relationship, even if the boy you like is really cute and nice to you. You are worth having someone who will respect you enough not to put you in a drama-filled situation. Why is it drama-filled? If his girlfriend finds out about you, it can create problems, and even worse, a fight could happen. This situation has too many opportunities for drama. You are a diva and divas do not subscribe to drama. If and when he breaks up with his girlfriend, and if you are available, date him and see where it goes. Remember, you are priceless and worth love, respect, honesty, friendship and a single boyfriend. Before you make a decision, put yourself in the other person's shoes and ask yourself, how you would react? Always remember that the choice is yours, and make a priceless decision because you are PRICELESS.

Let us know how it turns out and remember: you are PRICELESS, whether single or in a relationship.

I really want a tattoo, but my mother said I was too young. I am 16 years old and I know I am ready for one. My friend's brother is willing to do it for me, and I am thinking about going against my mother's wishes, but I am scared. What should I do?

Hello, Priceless. One. The great thing about a tattoo is that they are permanent; the bad thing is that they're permanent. Tattoos are not going anywhere. Before you know it, you will be at an age and in a situation where you can make that decision for yourself. At this time, you are not there. Give it time. If you really want one, waiting for it will be good. Trust me; it will be worth the wait for when the time is right and your mother is in agreement.

Listen to your fear. Your body reacts with fear because it is going into the protection state and warning you of danger. At times, we must listen to our body, especially when it is saying that it is scared. Take your body's warning sign and run the other way (smile). The decision is yours to make, but it is always wise and a priceless decision to listen to your mother, even when you disagree. One last point: When you do get the tattoo, make sure you go to a professional tattoo artist, because you want it done right, especially since it is going to be permanent.

Let us know how it turns out and remember: you are PRICELESS with a tattoo or without one.

If you have questions or comments, please contact Master's level social worker Ruby Taylor at Project@PricelessProject.com . Visit us at http://PricelessProject.com and read more questions and answers; join our community.

ORGANIZATIONS EMPOWERING YOUNG WOMEN

www.ConfidencetoGreatness.org

www.PricelessProject.com

www.LoveIsNotAbuse.com

www.LoveisRespect.org

http://www.allykatzz.com

http://www.girlsinc-online.org

http://fullcirclesusquehanna.blogspot.com

http://www.ywca.org

http://www.girleffect.org/

http://www.purplewings.org

http://evescircle.org/

http://www.girlology.com

http://seebeautiful.com

http://alwayssistersforeverbrothers.com

http://sisciety.com

http://www.brotherhood-sistersol.org

http://www.nextstepu.com

http://www.girlsguidetoswagger.com

http://www.girlsforachange.org

http://kidsrelaxation.com/

http://www.gems-girls.org

http://vintage.gurl.com

YOU ARE PRICELESS PROJECT

Write down and/or draw what makes you PRICELESS. If you are having problems writing or drawing something, please go back and see what you listed as your valuables, your riches and your circle of trust, and then list your accomplishments and failures. You are PRICELESS because of the good and bad. Remember, you are alive; and for that reason alone, YOU ARE PRICELESS.

HEALING ART JOURNAL

This is your place to draw, write, scribble, color, and/or create whatever is in your heart and on your mind. I am truly sorry for the bad things that happened in your life, but I am happy for the good things that I see in your life, now and in the future. When you know your self-worth, great things happen. I am celebrating those great things for you now!

Notes

Notes

COPYRIGHTED MATERIAL

CONTRIBUTORS

We would like to acknowledge the many publishers and individuals who granted us permission to reprint the cited material.

"Queen" reprinted by permission. © 2011 Kimberly Gray

"Through The Storm" reprinted by permission. © 2011 Melissa Carter-Coleman

"Hurt and Pain" reprinted by permission. © 2011 Nicki Higgins

"Still Striving" reprinted by permission. © 2011 Shanta Whitaker, Ph.D.

"My Education is Priceless" reprinted by permission. © 2011 Sylvia Morris

"Does He Know His Own Worth?" reprinted by permission. © 2011 Chelsa Brown

"You're Precious" reprinted by permission. © 2011 Shawn Kwadena Brown

"Life for Me Ain't Been No Crystal Stair" reprinted by permission. © 2011 Lucinda Lumpkin

----

Give the gift of "Confidence to Greatness for Teenage Girls" to a girl, young woman, relative, friend, or student you know.

With every book you purchase, you will help Confidence to Greatness provide free workshops and books to teenage girls in urban communities.

Check your local bookstore or order here.

YES, I want _____ copies of *Confidence to Greatness for Teenage Girls* at $16.97 each.

The Power of One	1 Book	$20.96
Dynamic Five	5 Books	$96.64
Ultimate Ten	10 Books	$191.24
Impact Twenty Five	25 Books	$475.04
Priceless Fifty	50 Books	$948.04
Influential One Hundred	100 Books	$1894.04

Included in the price above is $3.99 shipping and handling for one book and $1.95 for each additional book. Pennsylvania residents, please add 6% sales tax. Orders are shipped only in the United States. Payment must accompany orders. Allow two weeks for delivery.

Please turn page for order form

My check or money order for $_____ is enclosed.

YES, I want ____ copies of *Confidence to Greatness for Teenage Girls*

Name_____

Organization _____

Address _____

_____

City/State/Zip_____

Phone _____

Email _____

Make your check payable and return to:

Confidence to Greatness

917 Columbia Ave.

Suite 123

Lancaster, PA 17603

(866) 772-6299

www.ConfidencetoGreatness.org

Made in the USA
Lexington, KY
26 March 2013